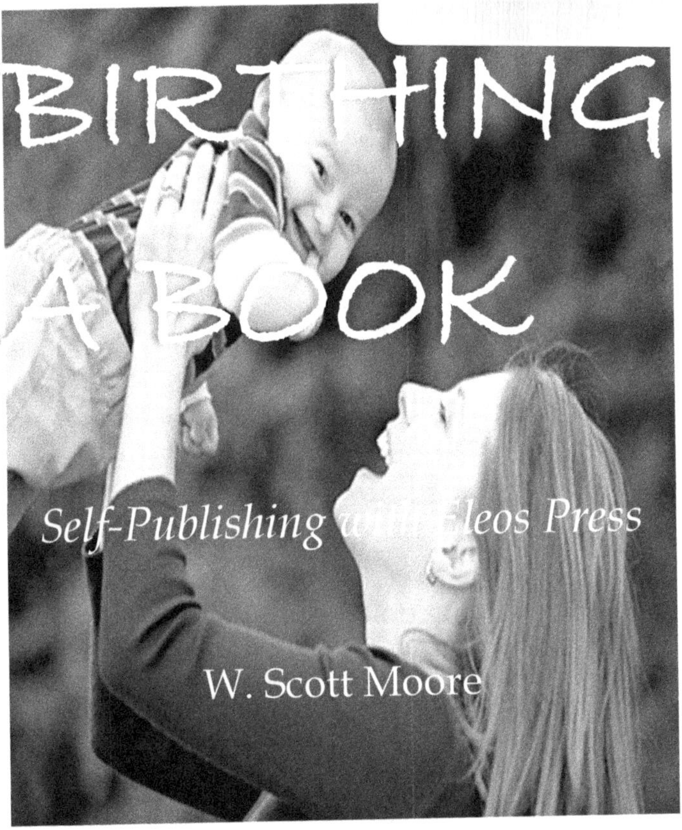

BIRTHING A BOOK

Self-Publishing with Eleos Press

W. Scott Moore

Eleos Press

Rogersville, AL

Third Printing, 9-5-2015
Birthing a Book

Author: W. Scott Moore
© 2014 by W. Scott Moore

Cover Design, Interior Formatting: Eleos Press
www.eleospress.com

ISBN-13: 978-1503392953
ISBN-10: 1503392953

INTRODUCTION

I Have Been There… I Understand

- Someone has said, "Ideas are like children — your own are wonderful." Your book is your **BABY**!
- You have been **impregnated** by a thought. Not a "hmm?" thought — an all-consuming thought that just will not let you go!
- For you, writing has become a **necessity** — you **have** to do it!
- You have literally had an out-of-body experience!
- Your "baby" — your book — is in one of the following stages of completion:
  - ✓ You have **conceived** it
  - ✓ You have begun to **nurture** it in the "womb" of your mind and your soul.
  - ✓ Your book has now grown so large that it is making you feel as if you are going to **explode** in childbirth!

Your Consultant: Who I Am…

Scott Moore, a.k.a., W. Scott Moore

(the author's name on my books)

Education: I have earned an undergraduate degree in Business Administration from the University of Georgia in Athens, Georgia, and two postgraduate degrees from the Mid-America Baptist Theological Seminary in Cordova, Tennessee: a Master of Divinity and a Doctor of Ministry.

Publishing Career: I have published, fully formatted, designed the covers, and uploaded a total of thirty books in both paperback and e-Book formats, including numerous books for eleven other authors. I have designed and maintained a website for book promotion, and established an author page on Amazon.com™. I have participated and assisted in several training opportunities for beginning authors.

Current Ministry: In addition to my writing and publishing, I am currently serving as the senior pastor of Crooked Oak Baptist Church, a rural church in north Alabama.

Family Life: My wife, Diane, and I have three grown children and five grandchildren.

What is Eleos Press?

I wrote my first book, <u>Exit Wounds</u>, in 2011. The theme of the book is mercy. Having studied Greek during my seminary days, I selected one of the two Greek words for "mercy" — ελεοσ (Eleos). According to Strong's Concordance, "[Although] both words denote sympathy, fellow-feeling with misery, mercy, compassion, ελεοσ… manifests itself chiefly in acts rather than words." Eleos is, therefore, mercy in action.

After publishing my second book, <u>Supernatural Strategy</u> with a fellow self-publisher, I decided to try my hand at the process. After much trial-and-error and, honestly, more error than trial, I have mastered the arts of editing, layout, and cover design.

My desire is to assist you, the aspiring author, in the publication of your book.

What Others Have Said:

You've gone above and beyond in helping me get started as an author. I appreciate all the extra things you did while I was learning the ropes.

-Steven C. Ames, author

Eleos has been, and continues to be, such a tremendous blessing to me. Through Scott's help, I've published one book with more on the way. Scott's simple, yet very excellent approach to publishing made putting the thoughts God gave me in book form a very easy, inspiring, and enjoyable task.

Eleos is the only way for me to go for every writing project in the future. Every writer should have Eleos on his or her side.

-Antoyne L. Green, author and pastor

Thanks for your friendship and your help for this book (Gambling with Eternity: The Loser Wins!)

-Dusty McLemore, author and pastor

As a new author, I wish I had found Eleos first. I found the publishing process frustrating, intimidating and expensive; Eleos is just the opposite. An author himself, Scott eliminated all the "speak," and presented me with all I needed to know. Eleos does what it says it will.

Scott was great in all aspects of publishing, providing assistance and suggestions where needed; he made the experience a pleasant one.

Eleos makes it possible for anyone from any walk of life to be able to publish. One might think that, with the more-than-reasonable price, a lesser product might be produced. Actually, I've found the opposite to be true! The books produced by Eleos are more appealing than the ones published by the "big" publishing companies! The books are something I can be, and am, very proud of.

I am very satisfied with Eleos Press. I'm grateful for the talent, integrity, and ability of Scott Moore. I highly recommend them to you!

-Barbara McGreger, author and speaker

Books I Have Authored
With Eleos Press

Books I Have
Published for Other Authors

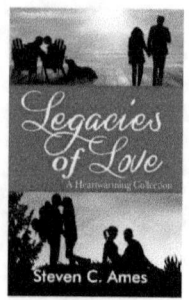

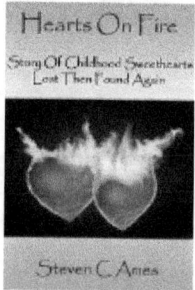

More Books I Have
Published for Other Authors

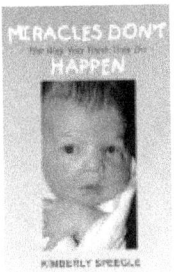

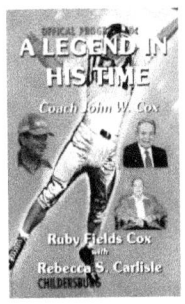

More Books I Have
Published for Other Authors

One Book I Have Fully
Edited for Another Author

Eight Reasons You Should Publish with Eleos:

1. I am a **midwife — I** have given birth to **nine** *children* (books) of my own and have assisted in the birth of **many** books for **several** other authors. As a result, you and I will be able to ride the **emotional roller-coaster** together. According to Elizabeth Eden, MD, in an article entitled "Understanding Psychological Changes during Pregnancy,"[1] we can anticipate the several **psychological changes** as we work through the process of publishing your book. Among those changes are:

   - *First Trimester: anxiety – You may not be able to see the changes that are happening during the first trimester, but they are significant. During this time, some new mothers might be filled with a feeling of anxiety about losing their new baby. These fears, though unfounded, are perfectly normal.*

---

[1] http://health.howstuffworks.com/pregnancy-and-parenting/pregnancy/issues/understanding-psychological-changes-during-pregnancy.htm, site visited on 3-18-2015.

- *Second Trimester: self-consciousness*, low self-esteem — Once the stress and anxiety of the first trimester have passed, the emotional changes of the second trimester begin. Though the feelings during this time will usually be less intense, they can be equally as troubling. Many mothers begin to feel self-conscious about the weight they are putting on to support their baby, and these feelings can lead to low self-esteem.

- *Third Trimester: fear* — In the third trimester, women are anticipating childbirth and coping with significant physical changes. While fears of losing the baby have usually disappeared by this point, a new anxiety takes its place -- the fear of the baby's arrival. Also, worries about labor and birth are also common during the last three months of pregnancy.

2. You will have full ownership of your book. If you allow me to become your consultant, your book will **always** be your book. I will simply help you in the process of "delivering your baby."

3. Through CreateSpace™, I will make your book available for sale through Amazon, Barnes and Noble, and other notable online retailers.

4. I will personally walk you through the publishing process, step-by-step, including:

   ✓ Formatting your manuscript into a standard size range: 5″ X 8″, 6″ X 9″, 7″ X 10″, 8″ X 10″, or 8 ½″ X 11″.

   ✓ Setting up an account with CreateSpace for publication of your book and to receive royalty payments from the sales of your book.

   ✓ Editing your manuscript for basic grammatical and spelling errors.

   ✓ Designing your book cover.

✓ Obtaining a free ISBN. "An ISBN uniquely identifies your book, and facilitates the sale of your book to bookstores (physical and digital) and libraries. Using ISBNs allows you to better manage your book's metadata, and ensure maximum discover-ability of your book."[2]

✓ Selecting your BISAC code. BISAC (Book Industry Standards and Communications) codes are a "standard used by many companies throughout the supply chain to categorize books based on topical content."[3]

✓ Determining the search words that will help potential readers in finding your book.

✓ Setting a reasonable price for your book.

---

[2]http://www.bowker.com/en-US/products/servident_isbn.shtml, site visited on 1/22/2014.

[3]   http://blog.wgeo.org/2008/02/20/what-is-a-bisac-code/, site visited on 11/22/2014.

✓ Establishing three discounts (10%, 15%, and 20%) that you will be able offer to family members, friends, and book retailers.

5. Revisions (within reason) are always free. If, say, a year from now, you would like to add a chapter, some pictures, readers' comments, or whatever—I will make those changes at no additional cost.

6. I will not only make your book available as a printed copy, but will also offer your book in an eBook form on Kindle™.

7. I am reasonably priced. From start to finish, I will only charge you **$399.00**.[4] There are absolutely **no hidden fees**.

8. You will pay **nothing** until you have a copy of your book in-hand, and are fully satisfied.

---

[4] I can offer a discount from the $399.00 price if you should choose to publish **either** a printed copy or an eBook (but not both).

INFORMATION

For more information about publishing with Eleos, contact me by email at:

moorescott@aol.com

View my books at:
http://www.eleospress.com